The Story of Cash Flow

A Commercial Folk Story

and

A Young Entrepreneur's Guide to Managing Money and Moneylenders

Or: How Cash Became King

by Steve Mullins

Published by
Ascot Associates Ltd

The Story of Cash Flow

First published in 2013 by Ascot Associates Ltd

ISBN 978-0-9576340-2-2

The contents of this slim volume are substantially the same as the Kindle version but with an added preamble that discusses why the book was written and a codicil that references Vladimir Propp – in a desperate attempt to pad it out a bit.

Contents

Preamble

For a variety of reasons I'm persuaded that I'm dyslexic and have great difficulty reading novels and writing coherently. The effect of this has been to cause me to explore several avenues in an attempt to better express myself.

One such avenue which was pointed out by my niece Lydia is the work of Vladimir Propp who dissected a good number of fairy stories and folk tales to recognise common characters and common threads that run through most of them.

For many years I have been a business advisor, ranging from start-ups to multinationals – all have the desire to do well yet many are held back by greedy self-interested people.

My intentions in writing this short book are twofold: to support business (and the budding entrepreneur) whilst at the same time learning to write a bit more fluently – it turned out to be much harder than I expected.

So here it is, The Story of Cash Flow, please enjoy it, feel free to comment and any comments used in future publications or editions will be gratefully acknowledged.

It might also benefit media studies pupils.

Enjoy

The Story of Cash Flow

A tale about managing finance

And the:
- *Pitfalls*
- *Charlatans*
- *Usurers*
- *Sluggards and*
- *Crooks*

Who add to the rich panoply that is today's competitive business

This book is written for all those people who:
- Are entrepreneurially minded
- Have an idea to take to market
- Are considering self-employment

A short story based on personal experience working with several hundred SMEs

In this short story you'll find some of the experience developed over many years with many businesses – whether established, or start-ups.

My goal is to help owner managers strengthen and develop their businesses in the face of the self-interested and greedy people trying to take it away from them.

I hope it helps you.

Acknowledgements

There are many people who have contributed to this tale, some knowingly and some unknowingly, and in particular:

Those many business owners and managers I have worked with and who taught me about some of the perils and pitfalls of managing finances in small organisations with very little in the way of buffers to tide them over financial difficulties or to manage the demands of an unhelpful bank.

Colleagues and friends who have helped to provide solutions to the situations those businesses found themselves in, and who have challenged, supported and helped develop my approach to business and, in particular, Peter Ainsley who has worked with me over many years to develop a fairly complete and dynamic model of joined-up management – of which finance is just one of the parts.

And last, but not least, family members (in alphabetical order) who contributed to the material, the structure and the editing:

Son Jonathan

Niece Lydia

Son Tom

None of whom take any responsibility for the contents of this story.

Thanks to you all.

Now on to the story proper

Dramatis Personæ

The Flow Family:

EBBAN FLOW – *Head of the family, manages the business*

BLODWEN FLOW – *Ebban's wife, oversees the family*

CASH FLOW – *Son, recently grown up*

Clients and Suppliers:

MILLIE ANAIRE – *Entrepreneur and philanthropist*

SLOWPAY & COMPANY – *A significant customer*

MR. RIVER – *Owner of the bank*

BEN FACTOR – *Money lender*

Professional Services:

GIL TEE – *Lawyer*

CON SULTANT – *Management advisor*

ANNETTE MARGIN – *Accountant*

The Villains:

PENNY PINCHER – *Head of the Pincher Family and friend of Mr. River*

MAX OVERHEAD – *Entrepreneurial member of the Overhead Brothers and owner of a pay-day loan company*

GENEROUS INVENTORY – *Badly controlled member of the Inventory Bunch and friend of Ben Factor*

The Minor Roles:

BART ENDER – *the pub landlord*

OLIVER SUDDEN – *the bailiff*

LAURA NORDER – *the police sergeant*

MARSHA LARTS – *the debt collector*

IGOR BEAVER – *the manager of the business in Knowledge*

SALLY FORTH – *the intrepid manager of the new franchise in Understanding*

Locations:

COMMERCE – *the country in which the story is set*

APPLICATION – *the town at the start of the adventure*

CHARLATAN – *a market town where the Chamber of Conmen is situated*

THE CHAMBER OF CONMEN – *a local networking institute*

USURY – *a small hamlet on the way from Charlatan to Knowledge*

KNOWLEDGE – *the town where Cash learns about business*

UNDERSTANDING – *the city where Cash learns about management*

FLOURISH – *a pretty village at the end of the adventure where everyone lives happily ever after*

NEVER-NEVER LAND – *a place where bills don't get paid*

All is Not as it Seems

Cash awoke with a start, he has a premonition this would be a strange day and sure enough, before the day was fully conscious, he found himself at the big table with the family in deep discussion about an unexpected adventure

The Flow family run a business by the River's Bank in a town called Application and together they enjoyed the social life; mother Blodwen, known to all as Blod, arranged dinner parties because she enjoyed cooking and entertaining, whilst father Ebban would lead the community singing and son Cash led the games and sports.

Ebban had decided to make the business more efficient and had bought a new system with a pre-payment made by Millie Anaire – a local entrepreneur and philanthropist; but she had subsequently cancelled the order to pursue a new opportunity.

The family had no idea how they could repay this debt and were afraid of being sued by the lawyer Gil Tee.

One saving grace was the significant debt owed to the family business by the Slowpay Company – a major client.

Blod was very concerned about the financial situation, even though Ebban was quite confident that the Slowpay debt would soon be paid – because he had sent them a reminder. Blod, however, was so anxious she that sent son Cash into the cut-throat land of Commerce to find fortune and a way to get the family business out of trouble.

The Adventure Begins

Cash set out for Knowledge and Understanding, two places where there were clever people who could provide advice and guidance; but, before setting off he had been warned not to travel through the market town of Charlatan where there were diversions and traps for the unwary.

But the way to Knowledge is long and winding, and Cash seeing a short-cut decided to ignore the advice and go via Charlatan, where he came across the Chamber of Conmen – a networking organisation where the Pincher Family, Inventory Bunch and the Overhead Brothers were meeting over supper; they invited Cash to join them and take up Membership.

As the evening slid gently into stories, reminiscences and song Cash found himself relating the story of the family business, how money had gone out from the business and a significant debt owed to the family had still to be paid.

This uncertainty had led to difficult times and the worry that the family might have to sell the business; so here he was – on his way to Knowledge to find a solution.

Penny (the head of the Pincher family) was a friend of Mr. River who owned the bank, she phoned Mr. River to advise him that there might be an opportunity to benefit from the Flow family's misfortune. The next day, Mr River went to see Ebban to discuss the situation.

The Bank Provides a Lifeline

After some deliberation, Mr. River resolved the situation by increasing the interest on a loan, reducing the overdraft facility, consolidating a number of accounts and providing emergency cover through a high interest credit card scheme.

Cash continued on his journey from Charlatan to Knowledge, happy to have met such nice people who had helped to get the family out of trouble. He was accompanied by Max Overhead who acted as a guide for a part of the journey and who had a pay-day loan business in Usury, a small hamlet on the way to Knowledge.

Meanwhile, Generous Inventory was dismayed that any commissions from Mr. River would be paid to the Pincher Family; so in a fit of pique he called his financial contact Ben Factor who met Cash just before the gateway to Knowledge.

Ben offered Cash funds against the outstanding bills from the Slowpay Company; Cash was pleased – he'd save on Mr. River's interest charges, and the Inventory Bunch were happy as they'd picked up a commission before the Pincher Family.

Ebban was delighted because here was another line of credit to tide the business over this difficult time whilst he waited patiently for the cheque from the Slowpay Company.

The family now had access to finance and as Cash entered Knowledge he thanked Generous and decided to take a well earned break there, in the sure knowledge that the family business was safe again.

Cash Launches His Own Business

That evening as Cash relaxed over a beer the pub landlord, Bart Ender, introduced Cash to Con Sultant – another traveller who he chatted to over the days and developed mutual trust; Con helped Cash to decide that it was right to set up a business in the Knowledge town centre.

Very quickly Cash's business became established. He used the hands-on experience he'd picked up working at the family business in Application and, with Con's support, the business was beginning to break even.

Unexpected Trouble

Then, out of the blue, the bailiff Oliver Sudden arrived to repossess Cash's horse; when Cash asked the reason, it transpired that Ben Factor, who was unpaid after three months by the Slowpay Company, had returned the unpaid invoices to Ebban, and demanded repayment of the money previously advanced, which was now outstanding.

Ben had also instructed the police sergeant Laura Norder to close the family business until the advance had been paid.

In order to forestall the bailiff, Cash remembered how helpful Max Overhead has been previously and took out one of his pay-day loans in order to gain some breathing space.

He temporarily closed the business in Knowledge and took Con, now a trusted advisor, to Application in order to see what could be done to put things right.

Deeper and Deeper

Back in the family business, Ebban continued to supply the Slowpay Company who had run up such a big debt on unrealised promises that it was now difficult to refuse delivery; the various loans had reached a level where the Flow company was working hard to service the interest never mind repay the principal, and the expensive new system was seriously under-used.

Cash didn't know which way to turn at first, but soon realised he needed to create a business plan to capture the issues and identify a workable way forward.

Con was introduced to the family and when he asked Ebban about the source of the problems Ebban told him about Millie cancelling a pre-paid order. It turned out that Con and Millie had been at college together so it was easy for Con to set up a meeting between Ebban and Millie.

A Rescue Negotiated

Millie, who recognised that successful businesses are mutually beneficial, negotiated to pay the Flow business a sum of money in return for equity – knowing that with Con to help there was every chance it would work out well for her.

Millie's money was used to pay down debt and allow Cash to hire an accountant, Annette Margin, to get the accounts back in order, provide controls & traceability and sort out the position with tax and rents.

And a Bonus

In addition, Annette identified a number of dodgy characters that were eating up profits and that Ebban could address, these included Re-work, Wastage and Staff-churn.

Cash, on Con's advice, spoke to Gil Tee about the legality of Mr. River's actions which he thought were highly dubious, and also instructed Gil Tee to take out a writ against the Slowpay Company to recover the money outstanding.

Gil successfully recovered most of the outstanding debt from the Slowpay Company and fined Mr. River for mis-selling financial instruments; he also recovered the bank interest overpaid by Ebban and obtained reparation for the damage to the business.

Meantime Annette had re-negotiated the rent which was adjusted favourably and re-cast the profit position so that the company received a significant tax rebate.

Con and Millie, who worked well together, joined forces to establish a business agency – Millie managed the selling, where she had some very good contacts, whilst Con managed the marketing.

The Flow company went from strength to strength, producing more and more product with less and less waste using the system bought with Millie's pre-payment; they undercut the competition and exported further and further afield. With few outside pressures Ebban could now concentrate on managing the business for optimum results.

Cash Develops The Business

Cash took an advance from the family and, with his embryonic business plan, returned to Knowledge with Annette and re-opened the business; Annette put in place the controls, budgets and management systems she had introduced to the family business, and set up the tax affairs to minimise payment.

Cash appointed young Igor Beaver to manage the business and used the money generated from fast stockturn, long creditor days, short debtor days and controlled materials management to fund a second branch in the city called Understanding.

This branch would provide a hands-off formula with the new controls and structure that would form the basis of a future franchised operation.

Cash introduced Annette to Max as the hero of the day; Max had got him out of a tricky situation and provided the means to return to the family business and help resolve the issues that were building up.

Max and Annette found they had a common bond in off-shore interests and got on well; in fact Annette was so impressed with Max socially that she agreed to settle down with him and they planned to marry.

Before long the trial franchise operation in Understanding was beginning to take shape and Cash was scouting around for a manager to develop this branch and consolidate his new business formula.

A Second Bombshell!

As the branch in Understanding was beginning to return a small, but regular, profit Max sent one of his debt collectors called Marsha Larts, to recover a significant sum that Max claimed Cash owed him.

This sum turned out to be the escalating compound interest from the pay-day loan that Cash had overlooked – and Max had deliberately not chased; biding his time until Cash's business had became viable.

Cash hired again Annette to look over the accounts to see where the oversight had occurred; Annette now realised how Max was using other peoples' ignorance to let interest build, in order to take advantage of them. She also recognised Max for the crook he was.

A Second Rescue

Cash, now growing in business confidence instructed Gil Tee to counter-claim against Max for an unlawful document; the counter-claim was successful and the details of the case published widely in the local press.

With the money from the settlement Cash was able to appoint an enterprising second manager – Sally Forth, to finalise the franchise in Understanding so he could enjoy a little time away from the business and take up golf again.

The franchise model became profitable and successful branches were being opened all over the Land of Commerce

The Story of Cash Flow

A Head Office and a Relocation

Cash, the family and close advisors moved from Knowledge and Understanding to a new head office in Flourish, a pretty village close to the family business in Application.

Cash Flow became Chief Executive – got his golf handicap into single figures, and became King of the business empire which he took to new territories with new products.

Ebban Flow stayed as Managing Director – became choirmaster, drove volume up and waste down whilst delivering increasing product volumes.

Blod Flow became Chairperson – gained her cordon bleu, and circulated throughout the organisations ensuring prudence and compliance across the business network.

Annette Margin became Finance Director – visiting the offshore places she enjoyed, and ensured the right controls were in place to maximise profitability, she also ensured these controls were kept properly up-dated.

Slowpay & Company recognised the importance of suppliers, mended their ways and became increasingly successful.

Max Overhead was shamed by the court case, and such was the local reaction he was banished to Never-Never Land.

But, sadly nothing could be done to curb the excesses of Mr. River or Ben Factor.

The Happy Ending

In the fullness of time there was a joint wedding when Cash married Annette and Con married Millie.

Cash and Annette continued to grow the business and enjoy the rewards of their labour.

Con was made professor of marketing and Millie received an honour for services to charity.

Con and Millie's agency thrived on the dividends from their equity stake in the Flow business and they went on to develop the agency by applying their joint skills to other organisations – but then, that's another story ...

And they all lived happily ever after

The End

Lessons Learned

A bit like the Victorian morality ending:

- Those who might appear at first sight as friends could be your enemies

- Good business decisions are helped with a reliable confidante

- If money is involved, those lending it will generally try to take advantage

- And above all – <u>Cash is King</u>

Moral

To get to Flourish you need support from appropriate trusted people to take you from Application, through Knowledge and Understanding whilst all the time avoiding Conmen and Usury.

The story as developed from Vladimir Propp:

Vladimir Propp analysed fairy stories and folk tales, and found that they all follow a similar pattern – a comparable journey is noted by Campbell in the **Monomyth**; however it is Propp's format that is used in The Story of Cash Flow

The Seven Characters:

THE VILLAIN – *Debt, represented by Slowpay and interest charges*

THE DISPATCHER – *Blod (Mother)*

THE (MAGICAL) HELPER – *Con*

THE PRINCESS, OR PRIZE – *Solvency; note also* THE FATHER, *paradoxically represented by Annette*

THE DONOR – *Millie*

THE HERO – *Cash, who is also* THE THREAD

THE FALSE HERO - *Max*

The Thirty One Functions:

ABSENTATION – *Cash leaves home*

INTERDICTION – *Don't go through Charlatan*

VIOLATION OF INTERDICTION – *Cash goes through Charlatan*

RECONNAISSANCE – *The banter at the Chamber meeting*

DELIVERY – *Cash describes the family situation*

TRICKERY – *Mr. River rearranges the accounts*

The Story of Cash Flow

COMPLICITY – *Max offers guidance to Knowledge avoiding usury*

VILLAINY OR A LACK – *Ben Factor demands payment*

MEDIATION – *The lack is made known by the bailiff arriving*

BEGINNING OF COUNTER-ACTION – *Loan from Max*

DEPARTURE – *Cash and Con set off for Endeavour*

FIRST FUNCTION (CASH IS TESTED) – *Creates the business plan*

HERO'S REACTION – *Negotiation with Millie*

RECEIPT OF MAGICAL AGENT - *Cash gets the money*

GUIDANCE – *With Con's help, Cash instructs Gil*

STRUGGLE – *Court cases*

BRANDING – *Cash devises an embryonic formula for managing business*

VICTORY – *Repayments and reparations*

LIQUIDATION – *The lack of money is resolved, family business solvent*

RETURN – *Cash returns to Knowledge*

UNRECOGNISED ARRIVAL – *Cash goes from Knowledge to Understanding*

PURSUIT – *Max sends debt collector for interest due*

UNFOUNDED CLAIMS – *Interest due is excessive*

RESCUE – *Annette identifies the issue, Gil rescues cash*

SOLUTION – *Max is sued and loses*

DIFFICULT TASK – *Cash establishes and proves the franchise model*

RECOGNITION – *The franchise model is taken up by others*

EXPOSURE – *Max's trial is high profile and widely published*

The Story of Cash Flow

RAPID RETURN HOME – *The family and advisors move together in Flourish*

TRANSFIGURATION – *Cash becomes CEO of all the family's businesses*

PUNISHMENT – *Max is banished*

WEDDING(S) – *Cash & Annette, Con & Millie*

A Little About the Author

STEVE MULLINS

Steve Mullins BSc, BSc, MCIM (Chartered), MCMI, FIC, FRSA developed his management perspective originally in major blue-chip companies in Research & Development and then in Brand Marketing. He now works in a self-employed role as founder and owner of Ascot Associates Ltd. He has been recognised as one of the best for Marketing Strategy and Business Planning in the south-east of England; he is also a Director of Business Wealth Ltd. where he is Programme Director for CMI Training.

After more than twenty years in blue chip organisations Steve has some twenty five years experience as a self-employed consultant working as a mentor, coach and strategist to Owner/Managers where he has been a part of the sustainability and growth of several hundred SMEs

Steve has also published, appeared on BBC Local Radio, teaches management and provides training in development and marketing.

Website http://manage4.wikidot.com/home
Blog site http://www.fundamentally.typepad.com/
Direct e-mail steve.mullins@virgin.net

The Story of Cash Flow

Steve is the Founder of Ascot Associates Ltd. A low profile, high performance organisation that delivers:

Marketing & Strategy
Training & Development
Coaching & Mentoring
Analysis & Improvement
Challenge & Support

Please contact Steve direct for more details.

Other publications

Redundancy
- A book about self-marketing: get a new job or get a better job, by Steve Mullins
ISBN 978-0-9576340-1-5

How Good Is My Glue?
- Non-financial due diligence, some of the things people might forget to ask
Steve Mullins and Peter Ainsley

How Near Is My Cliff-Edge?
- Five easy questions about the purpose of your business; ten searching answers
Steve Mullins and Peter Ainsley

Strategy
- Pitfalls and pathways
Peter Ainsley and Steve Mullins

The People in the River
- Twelve people you thought you knew
Steve Mullins and Peter Ainsley

Referral Marketing
- Turn your customers into your sales force
Vince Golder and Steve Mullins

Be the Consummate Professional
 - Tips on how to maximise your professional
   credibility, status and success
Vince Golder and Steve Mullins

All available on Kindle

And each for about the price of a cup of High Street
   coffee! – ***Brilliant value***

Ethical Crisis Management
 - How any decision, delayed long enough, will seem
   to be a good one
ISSN 1741-5187 – The International Journal of
   Management & Decision Making, Vol. 6 2005,
   pp.372 - 381 – available only from the publishers

www.ingramcontent.com/pod-product-compliance
Lightning Source LLC
Chambersburg PA
CBHW022058190326
41520CB00008B/806